Badgers

Badgers are mysterious countryside creatures with many habits which are almost human. They change their "bedding" of grass and straw regularly. They remain faithful to one mate, and keep their sets, or earths, well aired.

The author of this book looks at the lives and characters of these fascinating animals – what they eat, how they behave at breeding time, how the young are born and brought up. He shows how they pass the winter, tells of their odd burial habits, and examines their chances of survival in a threatening world.

This book contains more than 50 illustrations and has a glossary, a section on where to find out more, and an index.

Badgers

Alan Bartram

Priory Press Limited

Young Naturalist Books

Squirrels
Foxes
Bats
Rabbits and Hares
Hedgehogs
Frogs and Toads
Snakes and Lizards
Badgers
Deer
Spiders
Otters
Rats and Mice
Bees and Wasps
Stoats and Weasels
Pond Life
Crickets and Grasshoppers
Ants
Beetles
Birds of Prey

SBN 85078 179 5
Copyright © 1974 Priory Press Ltd
2nd impression, 1976
First published in 1974
by Priory Press Ltd
49, Lansdowne Place, Hove, Sussex BN3 1HS
Filmset by Keyspools Ltd, Golborne, Lancs
Printed in Great Britain at
The Pitman Press, Bath

Contents

1	Badgers of the World	7
2	Built for Digging	21
3	The Badger's Food	31
4	Mating	43
5	Family Life	57
6	Badgers and Man	67
	Glossary	76
	Finding Out More	78
	Index	79
	Picture Credits	80

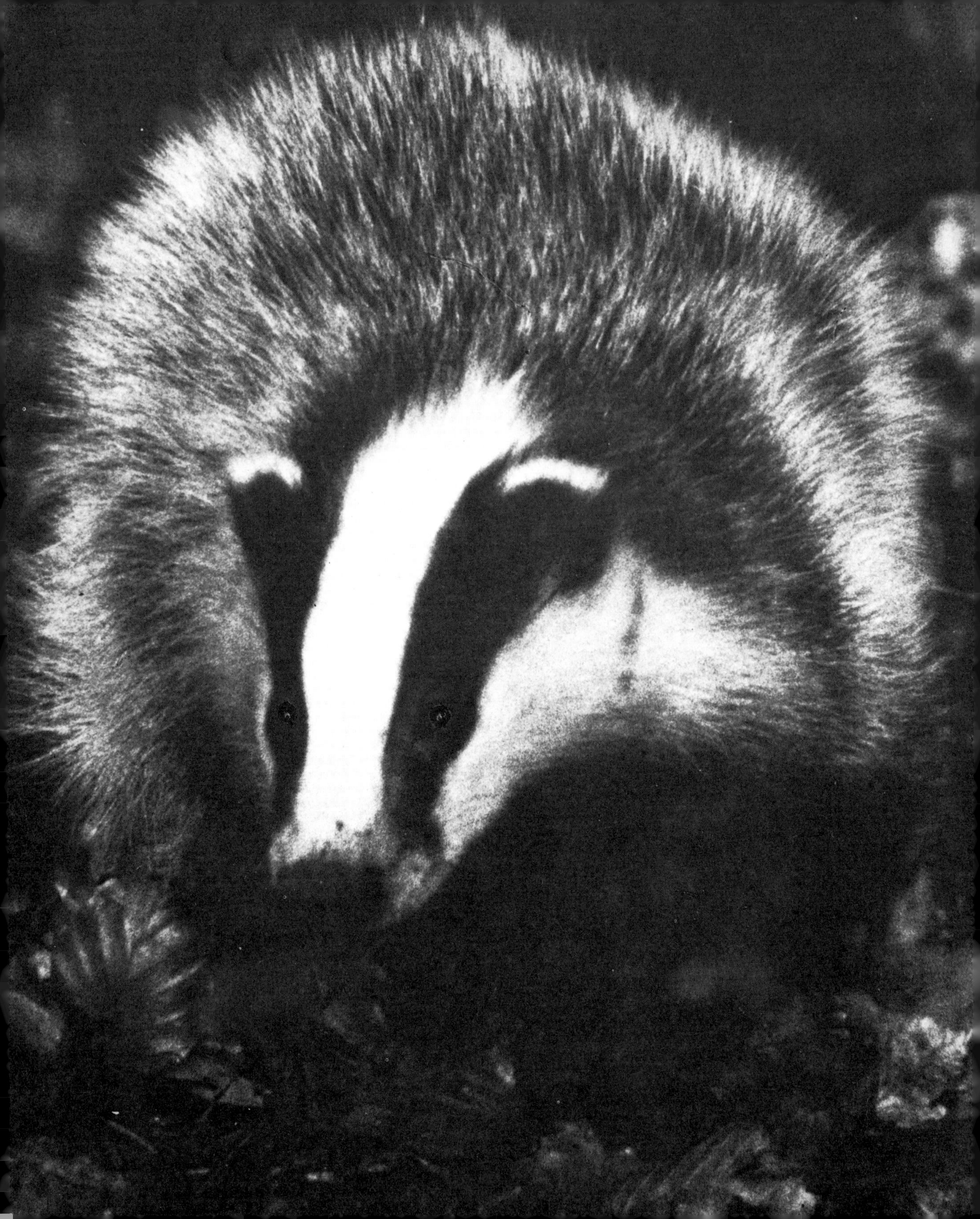

1 : Badgers of the World

With his striking markings and strange habits, the badger is one of the oddest creatures in the animal world.

Badgers belong to that great group of mammals, the Carnivores. As this name implies, the carnivores catch and eat living animal prey. Some badgers, however, have become omnivorous, eating both animal and plant food. Close relatives of the badgers are the stoats, mink, weasels, skunks and otters.

The fossil bones of badgers date back to the Pliocene period, about seven million years ago. Today there are many different kinds of badger, some quite unlike the

A European badger, *meles meles* in its Latin name, noses through the dusk in search of food.

Badgers of the World

European Badger we are familiar with. Badgers are found in North America and Asia, but not in South America.

The European badger is the only one which lives in Great Britain. It is found throughout Europe wherever the countryside is hilly and wooded. It lives as far south as Israel, Iran and Southern China, and as far west as Japan.

There are badgers in almost every county of Great Britain. They are most common in the West Country and the Welsh border lands. They are much rarer in East Anglia, where there is always a danger of flooding. You will not find them in the Pennines, Scottish or Welsh

A skunk (*right*), the badger's close American relation, has a brief meeting with a racoon.

Other animals which are closely related to the badger: the weasel (*above left*), the stoat (*above right*), and (*below*) the otter.

Badgers of the World

The ratel or honey-badger is usually grey or white above and black below. It ranges from India to Africa, south of the Sahara.

Highlands, probably because there is not much food there for them.

The Stinking Badger lives on the islands of South-East Asia – Java, Sumatra and Borneo. It spends a lot of time digging after worms and grubs. Its tail is very short and its ears very small. Its fur is brown, with a white stripe running from the head to the tail along the middle of its back. As its name suggests, the stinking badger gives off a powerful smell, probably for defence.

There are three kinds of Hog Badger. They are found in China and South-East Asia. They are called hog badgers because they have long, moveable snouts.

Asia also has Ferret Badgers. These are good tree-climbers, using their long, bushy tails for balance. They

Badgers of the World

American badgers are only distantly related to European badgers.

A pair of American badgers.

are sometimes very brightly coloured; one of them is black and orange, for example. They are carnivorous, feeding on insects, lizards, birds and their eggs.

Finally, there are the American Badgers, which live in North America. They too are carnivorous and inhabit open, sandy plains. The food they like best is the ground squirrel; one family of American badgers knew how to catch these by blocking up all the entrances to the burrows except the main one. They then dug down into the nest to catch the squirrels. American badgers also eat mice and insects.

The European badger is about three feet long from the snout to the tip of the tail. The tail itself is about four inches long. It usually weighs about twenty-five pounds, although sometimes they reach over forty pounds. As we shall see, badgers are very strong animals. They can dig well and their bite is very powerful.

Ground squirrels, much liked by American badgers. They eat both animal flesh and natural vegetation.

Above: A badger leaving its set. Its markings show up clearly in the dim light.
Right: From a distance its back is grey, but in fact each hair is white.

The most striking thing about the European badger, looking at it, is its markings. The back of the animal looks grey; but each hair is white, with a black area in the middle. The fur is much darker on the underside and its legs are almost black. If we compare this with that of other animals we can see how unusual it is.

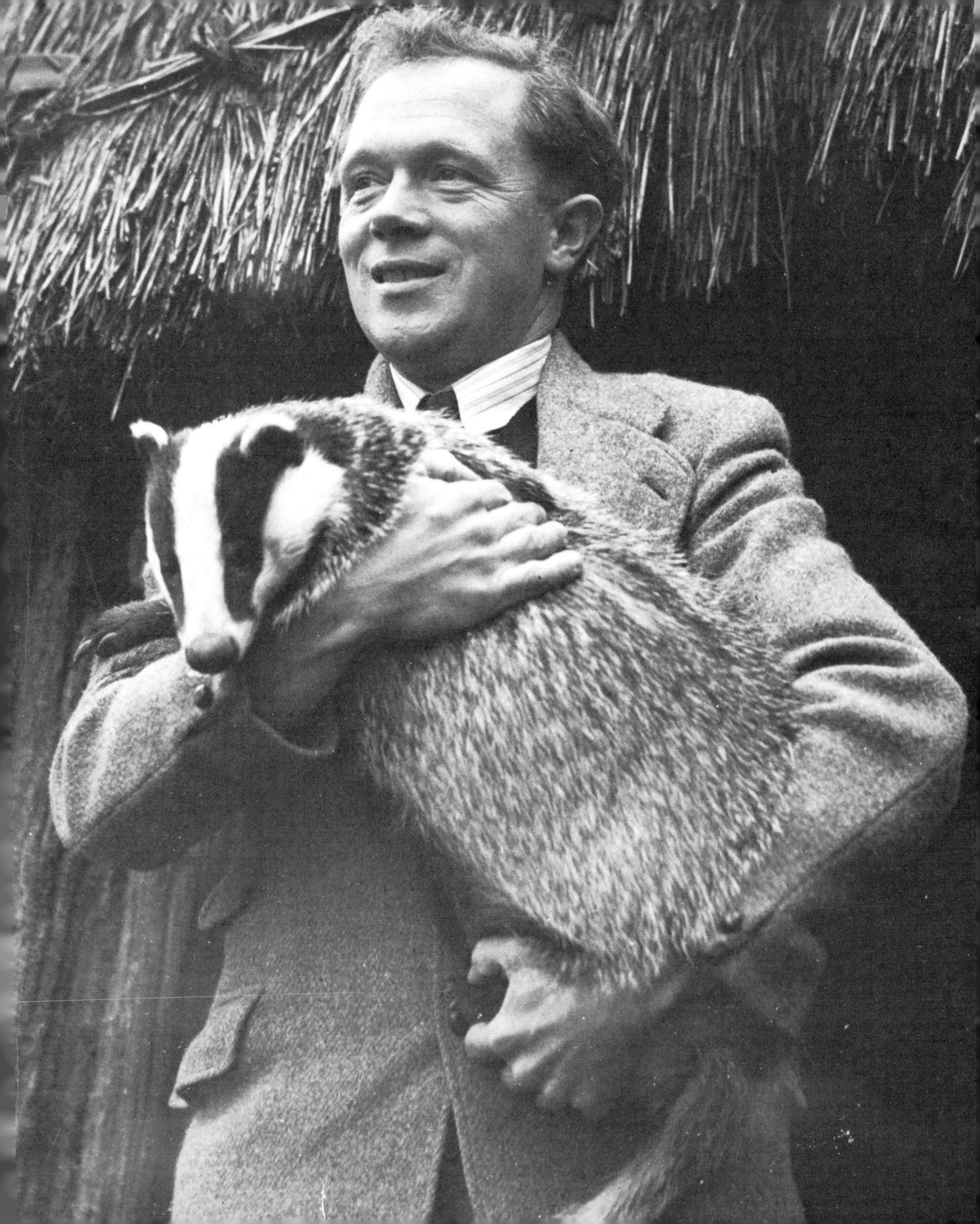

Badgers of the World

Most animals are marked so that their enemies find it hard to see them. If they are carnivorous, they do not want to be seen by their prey either. Since sunlight shines from above, it lights up the back of an animal, but leaves the belly dark and shaded. A dark underside looks very obvious against a light background. For this reason, many animals display what is called *countershading*. The hair on their bellies is much lighter than it is on their backs. Think of a rabbit, deer or fox. In this way the brightness of the animal is evened out.

But the badger is just the opposite; its back is much lighter than its belly. It seems as if the badger is trying to make itself look obvious. The badger's head too looks very obvious. Most of it, including the tip of the ears, is white, but two black stripes run back from the snout past the eyes and ears. This striping makes the badger the easiest British mammal to see in dim light.

Why should the badger want to be so easily seen? If we look at other animals, we find that very often those that are striking to look at have good defences. The black-and-yellow striped wasp has its sting, and the bright red ladybird beetle has a nasty taste. We say that these animals display *warning coloration*; other animals soon learn to keep away.

The badger too has a powerful defence: its bite. It is very strong indeed, and because of it the badger has no enemies except man. So it seems that the badger's black

Right: The badger's brightly marked head is a warning to others to keep away: he has a powerful bite.

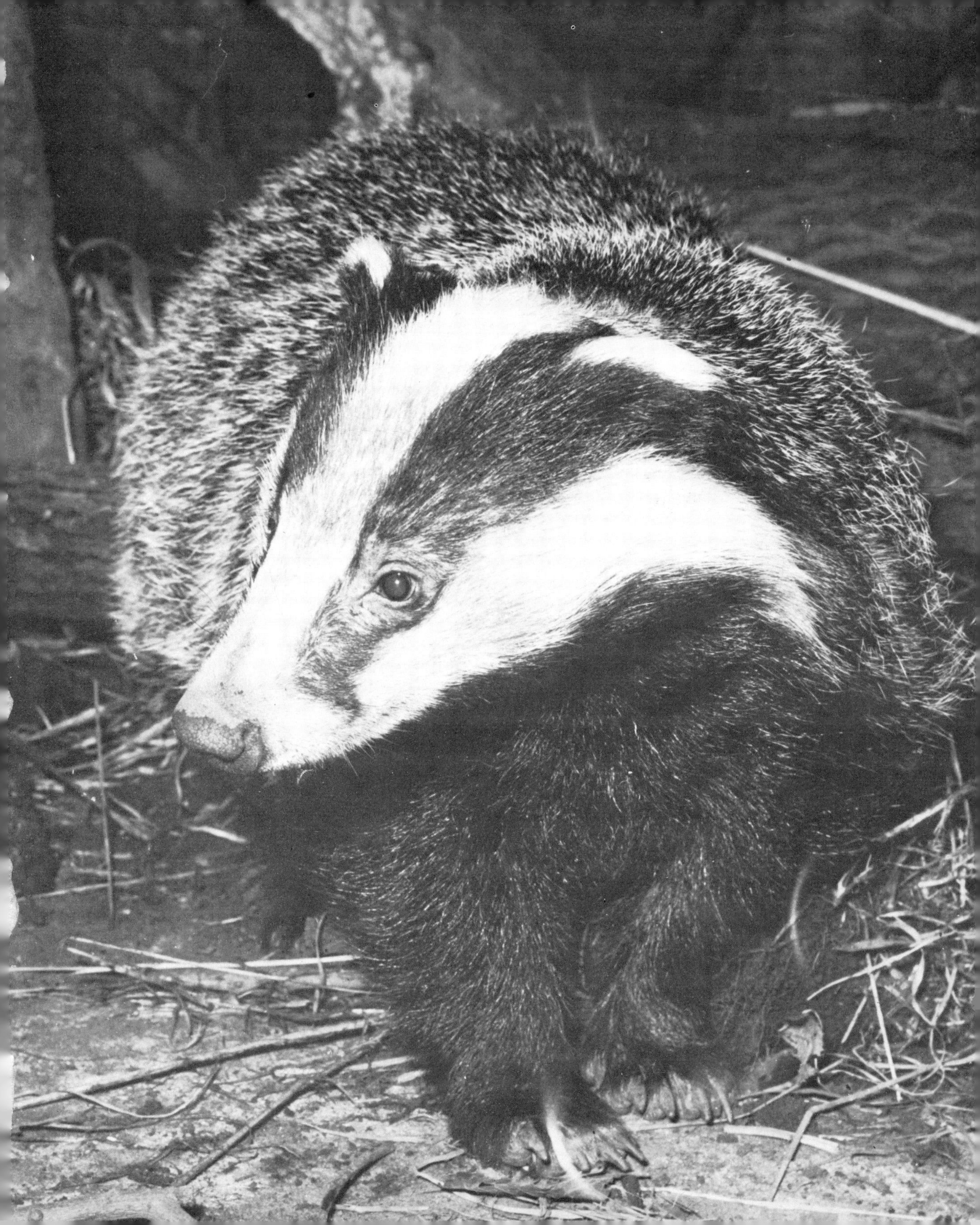

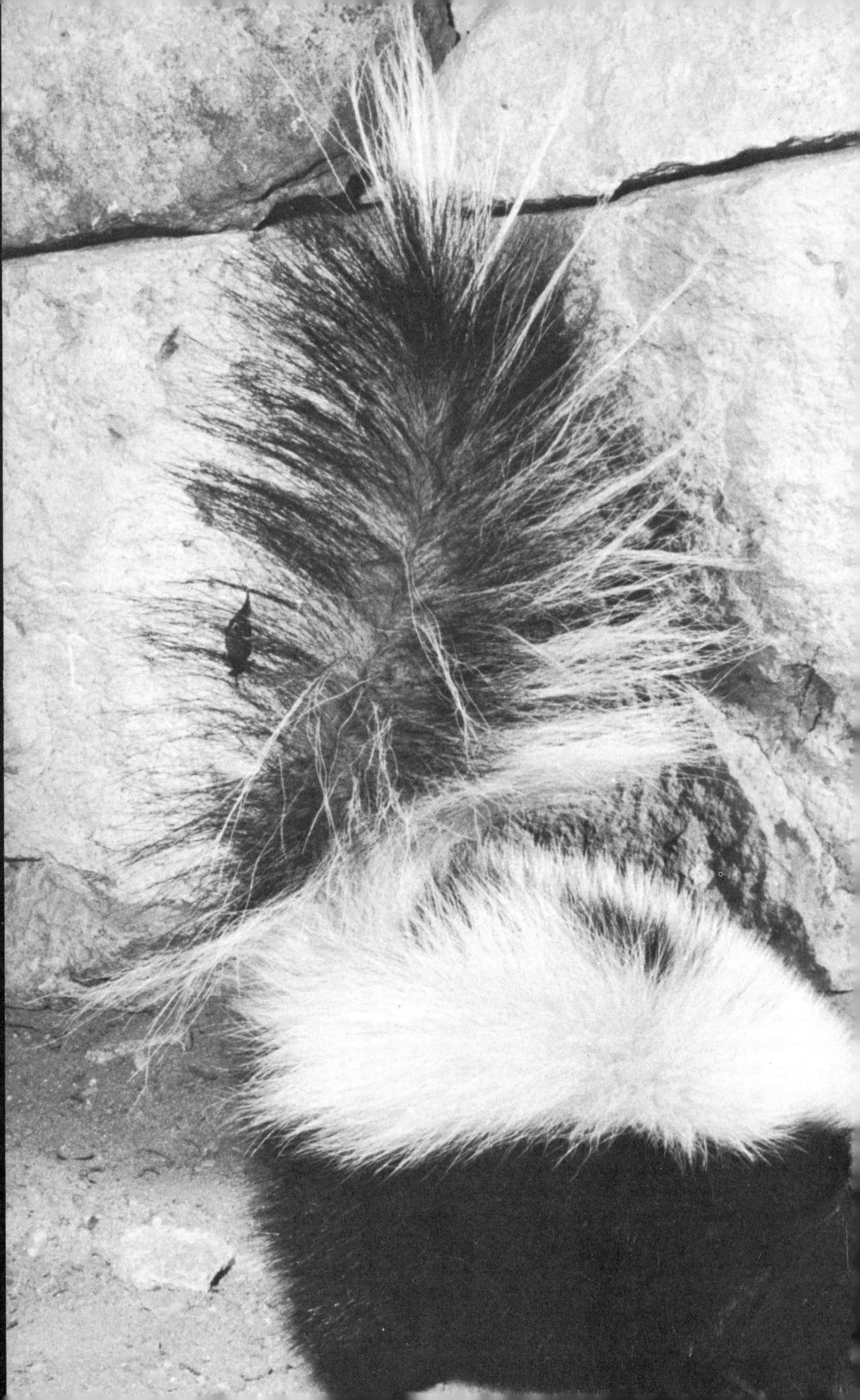

The badger's relative, the skunk, also has warning coloration. Its weapon is a nasty and strong-smelling liquid which it squirts at enemies.

Badgers of the World

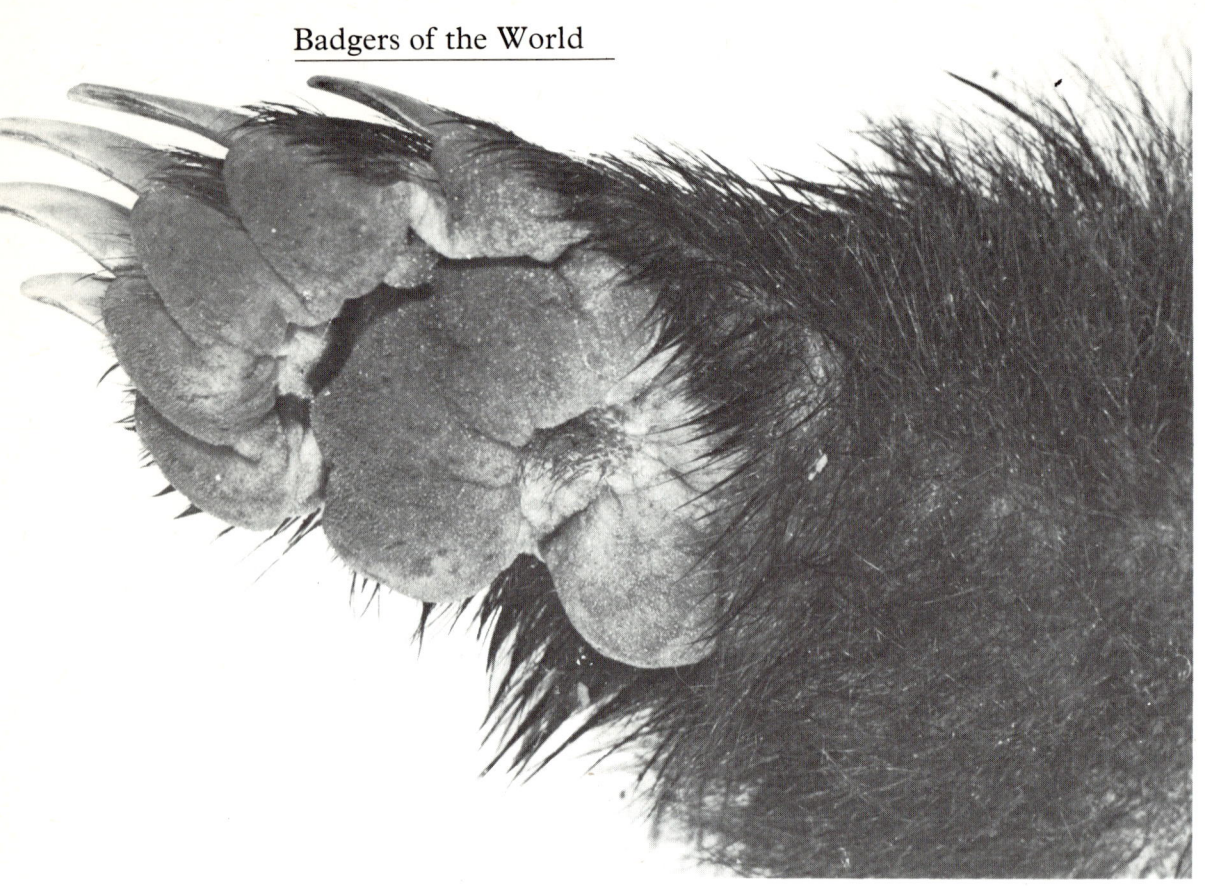

The badger's paws are made especially for digging: their ankles are strong and their claws long and tough.

and white stripes are a warning to others to keep away. The stinking badger too has warning coloration; it has a white stripe running along the middle of its back. Its defence is the unpleasant smelling liquid which it gives off from a gland beneath its tail when it is attacked. Weasels, stoats and polecats too give off a bad smell. But of course the skunk, another close relative of the badger, is worst of all. If disturbed, it will turn around, raise its tail and squirt a yellowish liquid with such a sickening stench that it overpowers any attacker.

2: Built for Digging

The word badger probably comes from a French word *bêcheur*, meaning digger. Badgers are very powerful diggers; they move vast amounts of earth to make their underground homes, called *sets*. Their leg bones are very sturdy and their ankle joints are specially strengthened

Badger sets. Each set has several entrances and airholes.

There is normally a "slide" at each entrance to the set, which can be up to 16½ feet deep.

for digging. Their claws are very stout and long; they keep them sharp by scratching them down the trunks of trees near the set.

Badgers are nocturnal animals; they feed at night and spend the day in their sets. Sets last for many years, and so few badgers have to dig a set from scratch. They usually enlarge and clean out old sets or sometimes rabbit warrens.

A badger at work, digging hard.

Badger's sets are usually dug where there is plenty of cover, especially in woods. If they can find a slope to dig into they will use it.

Sets can be very big indeed. The biggest ones have about fifty entrances, and their tunnels may be over a hundred yards long. Sets are usually dug in soft ground such as sand or chalk, which is easier to dig. The soil that has been dug

Built for Digging

out is made into a huge pile outside the set. At various places along the tunnels are sleeping and breeding chambers.

Living in large sets poses problems. The first is ventilation; when many badgers are sharing a set, the air is likely to become foul. For this reason they build the tunnels level, parallel with the ground, so that there are no deep places where bad air can settle. They also make small air holes in the tunnels, hidden by a few twigs.

The second problem is sanitation and hygiene. The badgers would soon foul up the set with their droppings, and for this reason they dig shallow dung pits close to the entrances to the set. If you find fresh dung in these pits it means that badgers are using the set and are likely to be about. The badgers' only enemy, apart from man, is disease. Tonsilitis, and sometimes mange, are diseases deadly to badgers. But we can be sure that far more badgers would fall ill and die if they did not keep themselves and their homes as clean as they do. The chambers in their sets are lined with bedding; this is usually straw, grass or bracken. The badger brings it to the set between its front paws and chin, shuffling backwards, and lines the breeding and sleeping chambers. Most of the bedding is brought in autumn and dragged out and changed in spring. The bedding is changed regularly throughout the year, however; by throwing out the old bedding the badgers also throw out the eggs of parasites such as fleas and mites (the badger's flea is the same one as the human flea!).

Right: Badgers dig with their heads as well as their paws. This one is using his snout as a shovel.

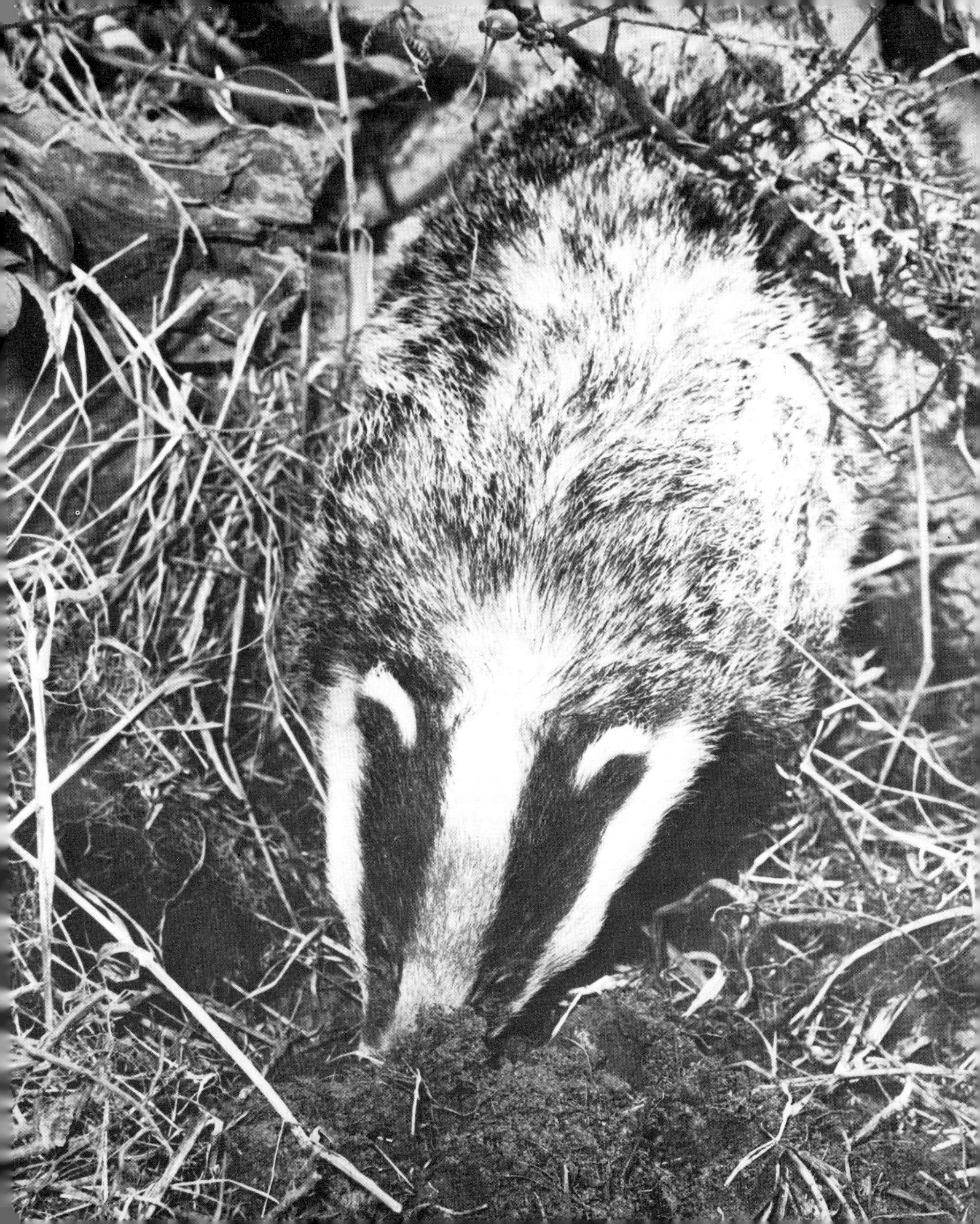

A badger with his nose still dirty from digging with his snout.

Also, badgers use only part of a set at one time; they often move on to a cleaner part.

We have seen that badgers are active at night. Because of this, and because they live underground, we expect their senses other than sight to be well-developed. Badgers indeed cannot see very well. Like many other animals, like foxes, they can only see an object when it is moving. As long as the wind is blowing your scent away from them, you can sit watching badgers without their noticing. But if you make the slightest move they will disappear into their set.

A badger returning to his set.

Built for Digging

Above and right: Badgers have a very strong sense of smell, and they rely on it as much as we do on our sight.

The badger's sense of smell, and hearing too, is excellent. They must recognize each other underground by scent. Badgers know that there are enemies about, and where they are, by smell. It is quite useless to hide near the entrance of a set at night, hoping to see badgers, if the wind is blowing your scent towards it. One of them will

Built for Digging

Built for Digging

come to the surface, sniff the air once, and disappear. As we will see, badgers also use their sense of smell to find food, especially if it is beneath the soil.

There is one more problem to do with living underground. What happens when a badger dies? The dead badger is a danger to health. Someone has suggested that badgers die at the end of a tunnel in the set. They are then walled up by other badgers. Much later, another badger may burrow to enlarge the set and come across the bones. It clears these out, and for this reason you can sometimes find a badger skull at the entrance to the set.

But one naturalist witnessed an amazing "funeral." He saw a female appear at the set entrance and utter the blood-chilling cry that badgers give. She then went a short distance away and spent some hours digging a large hole. She was joined by a male, and together they pushed and dragged out a dead badger from the set. The dead badger was the sow's mate. They pushed it into the hole and covered it with earth. The sow then went back to the set and her helper disappeared.

Right: A badger eating roots.

3: The Badger's Food

Although badgers belong to the carnivore group of mammals, not all of them eat only animal food. The European badger is, like ourselves, omnivorous; it eats both plants and animals.

The badger's teeth are certainly those of an omnivorous mammal. In flesh-eating carnivores, such as wolves and

Feeding off the remains of a young rabbit.

foxes, the back teeth are shearing blades which chop the food up. But in the badger these teeth are much flatter, for crushing up plant food.

Badgers eat a lot of fruits and seeds in the autumn. These include acorns, blackberries and apples. During this time too, badgers dig up the underground storage organs of plants, such as bluebell bulbs, and roots and rhizomes. In

They also like milk and, like hedgehogs, can be lured by a dish of it left at a convenient placc.

the spring, the sap rises in the trees to feed the bursting buds. So badgers sometimes strip off the bark of sycamores or beeches and lick the sweet, sappy wood underneath. They will also eat grass, leaves, and even fungi.

Worms are probably the favourite food of the badger. They are specially easy to catch when they are lying on wet ground after heavy rain. One badger, which had been

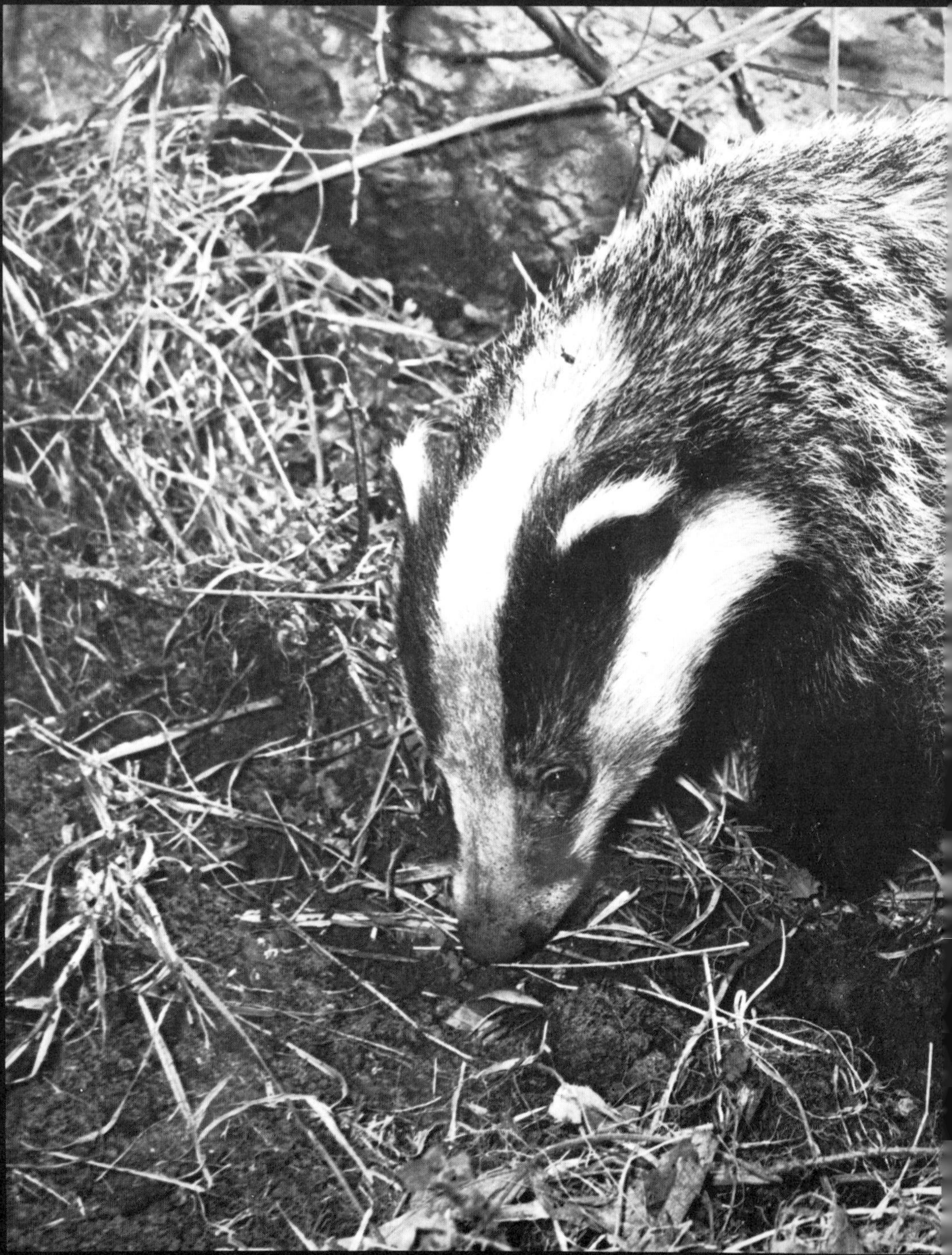

Starting to dig.

The Badger's Food

killed by a car, was found to have over three hundred worms in its stomach.

They also eat beetles with relish, especially the big black Dor Beetle. These and other beetles are found under cow dung, which the badger turns over with its paws. Badgers also eat caterpillars which feed at night on leaves within reach of its jaws. They crunch up slugs and snails too; a badger was once seen climbing a tree in search of slugs.

Wasps and bees are a special delicacy for the badger – a wasps' nest has fat grubs, and a bees' nest has honey. If a badger discovers a bees nest, it takes no notice at all of the hundreds of angry insects that swarm around it. The badger furiously digs into the nest, eating up the honeycomb and snapping at the bees. The bees attack the badger, but their stings have no effect. This is because the badgers skin is too thick; but if a bee does sting a sensitive spot, the badger feels it and runs off!

Among larger animals, young rabbits were probably most often eaten by badgers, at least before rabbits were almost wiped out by myxomatosis. Adult rabbits move too quickly for the badger, although it will eat them if they are caught in traps. The badger can smell the rabbits in their underground nests. To reach them, it does not use the main entrance to the burrow but simply digs straight down to them. Badgers also eat plenty of rats, mice and voles.

Right: Nosing through dead leaves and sticks in search of slugs and worms.

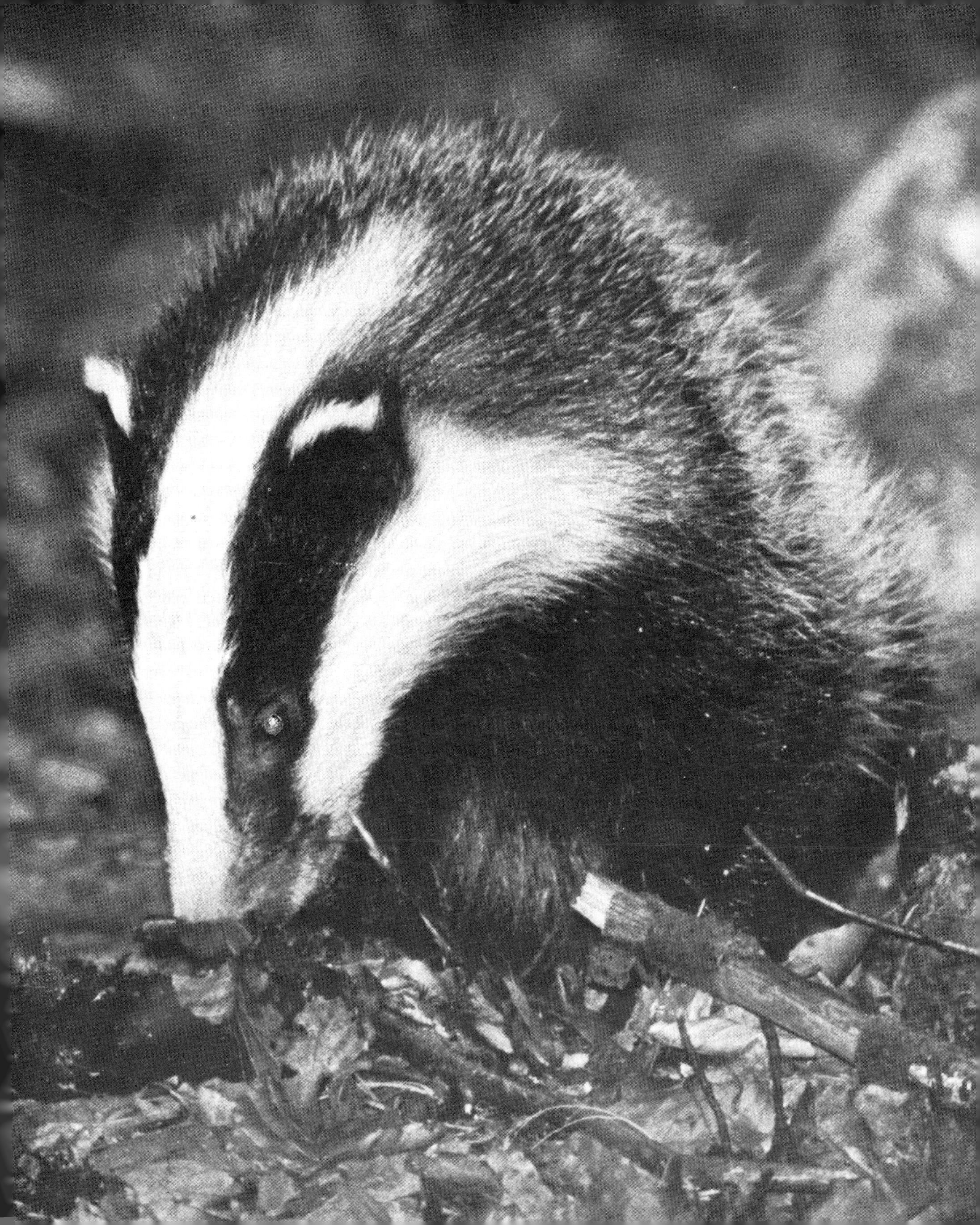

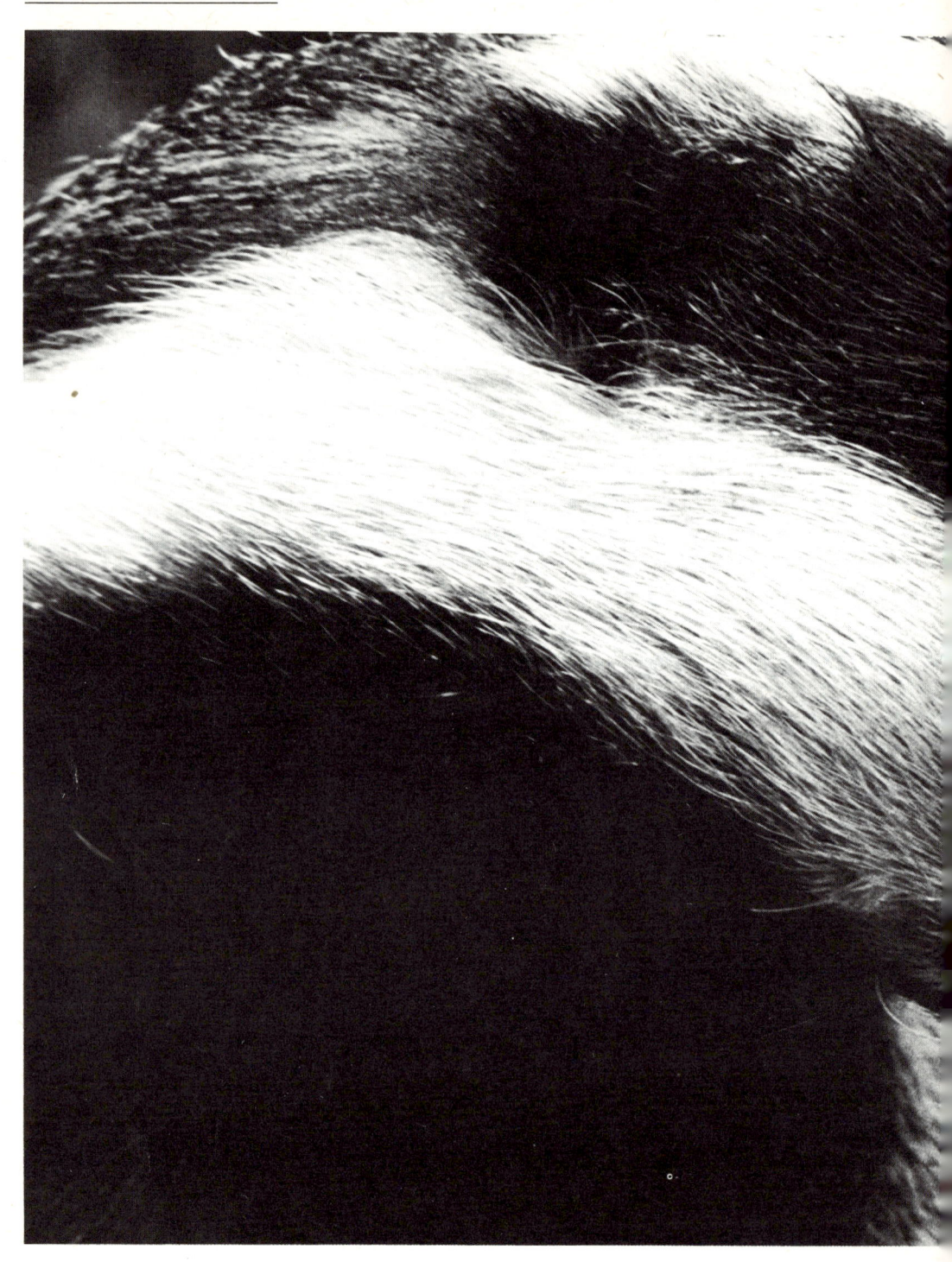

The Badger's Food

38

The Badger's Food

A close-up of a badger's head shows its long and powerful jaw.

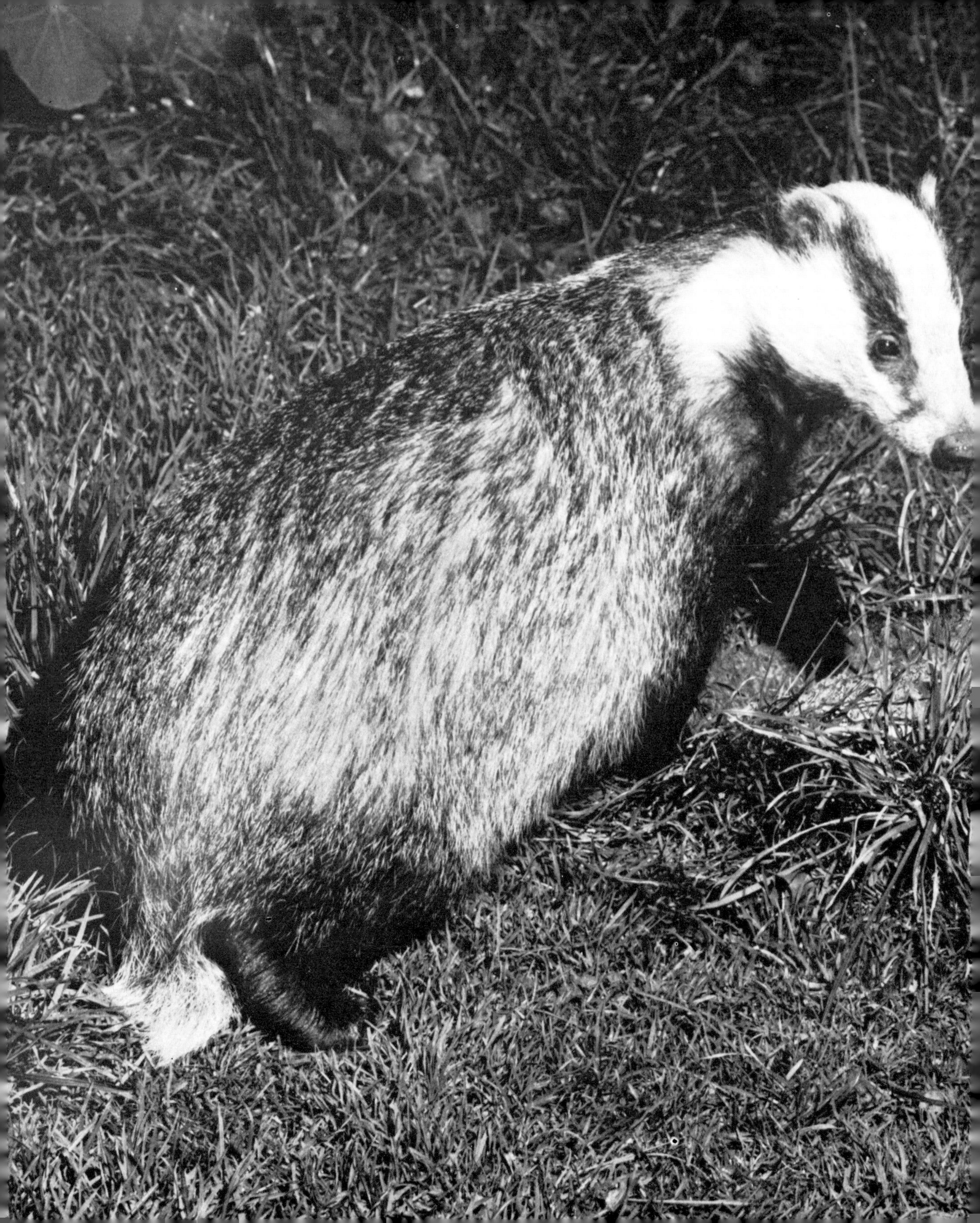

The Badger's Food

Hedgehogs too form part of the badger's diet. We don't know how the badger manages to unroll the animal, but once it does it eats it belly first, skilfully avoiding the spines. Only four spines were found in the stomach of a badger that had eaten four hedgehogs.

Badgers have a reputation for killing lambs, but this is very, very rare. Sometimes a dead lamb is found at the entrance of a set, but badgers never drag their food to the set. In fact the lambs are brought there by foxes, which sometimes share the badgers' home. Poultry may be attacked and eaten by badgers, but this too is very rare.

In comparison with the European badger, the American badger is mostly carnivorous. It eats ground squirrels, mice, insects and even the occasional rattlesnake.

Although the European badger eats only small animals and plants, it has an extremely powerful bite and sharp canine teeth. It uses these for defence; a dog is likely to come away badly mauled after fighting with a badger.

The badger's skull shows two features which have to do with its powerful bite. In most animals, including ourselves, you can dislocate the jaw – knock it out of its sockets – because the jaw joint is shallow. But in the badger the jaw joint is very deep and it is impossible to dislocate the jaw without breaking part of the skull.

Left: This narrow-striped badger has more white and less black on his head than others, making him show up even more.

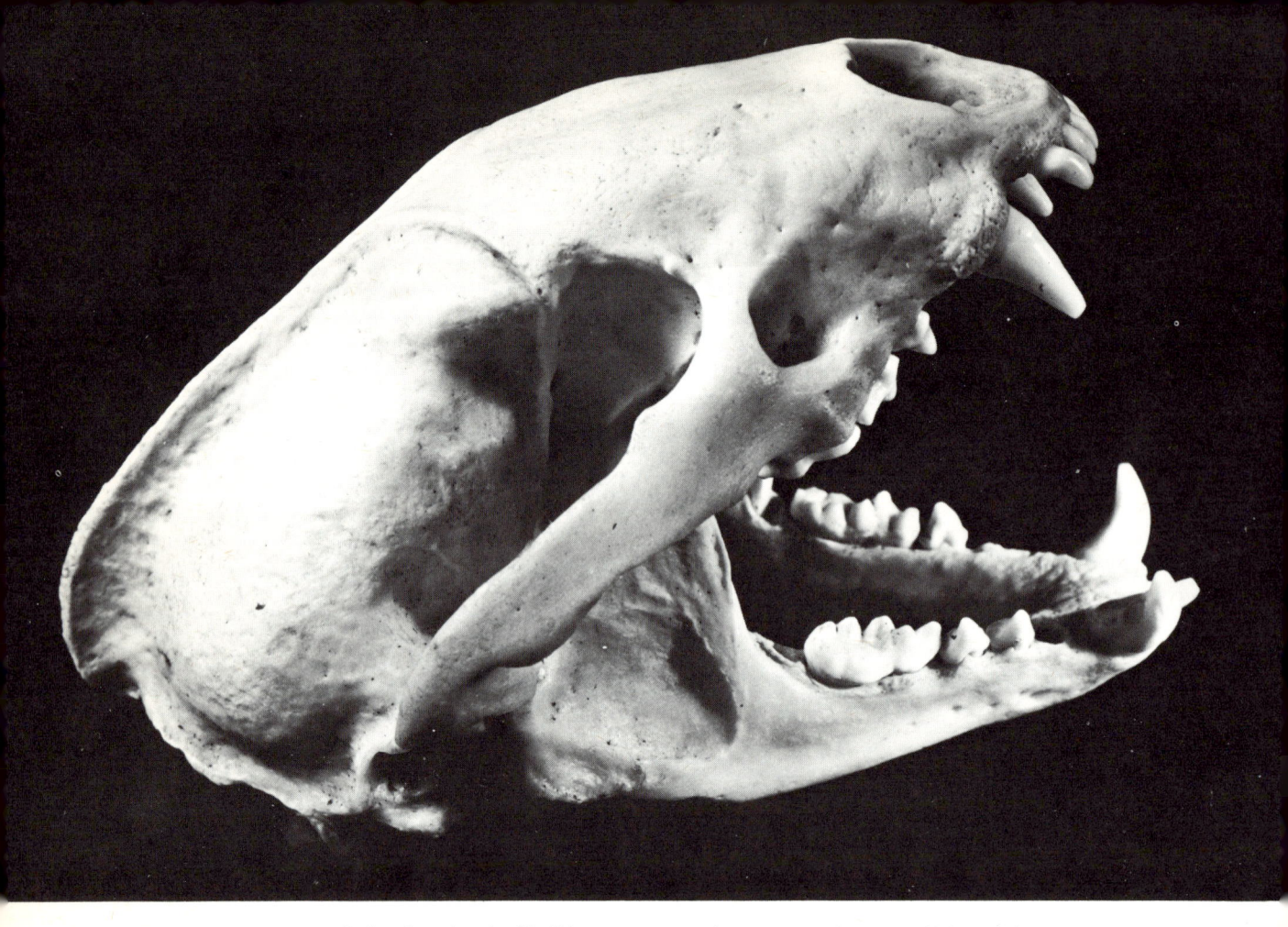

A badger's skull. You can see the strong jaw and the ridge on the back of the head which protects it; but the top and front of the head is weak.

The second feature of the skull has to do with the size of the jaw muscles. The larger the size of a muscle, the more powerful it is. The badger has a long tall ridge along the middle of the back of its skull. This gives a big area for the attachment of the large jaw muscle. Because of this ridge, it is difficult to stun or kill a badger by knocking it over the back of the head. But a blow to the snout, which is weakly protected, will kill it.

4: Mating

Badgers are family animals; the same pair of badgers mate and produce young each year. It is easy to tell the sexes apart. The male badger, or boar, has a wider head and thicker neck than the female (sow). Also the boar's tail is lighter in colour than the sow's.

Most pairs mate between July and mid-September. During this time there is great sexual excitement. The

A badger scratching itself.

Their eyes glow in the light of the photographer's flashbulb like a cat's or dog's.

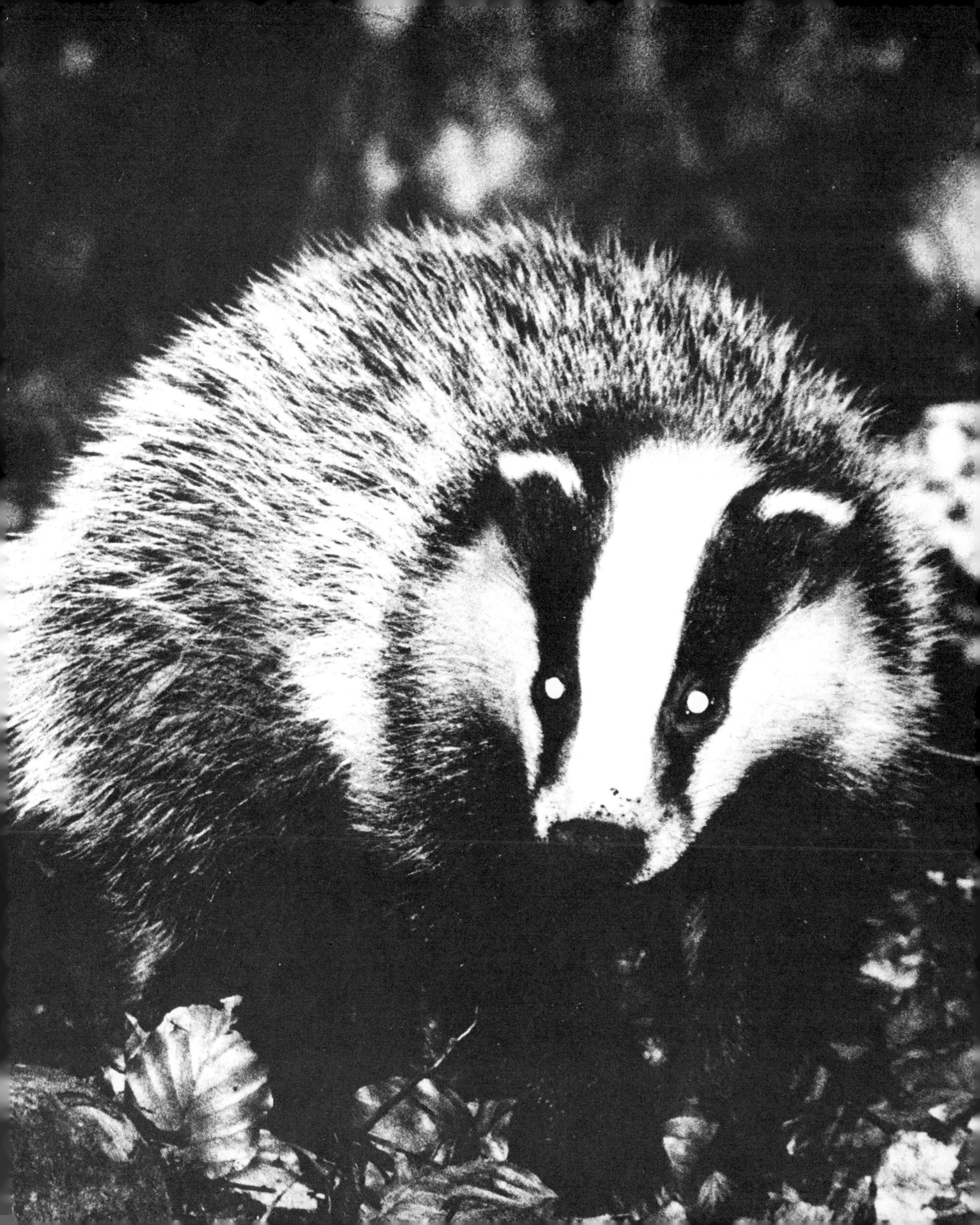

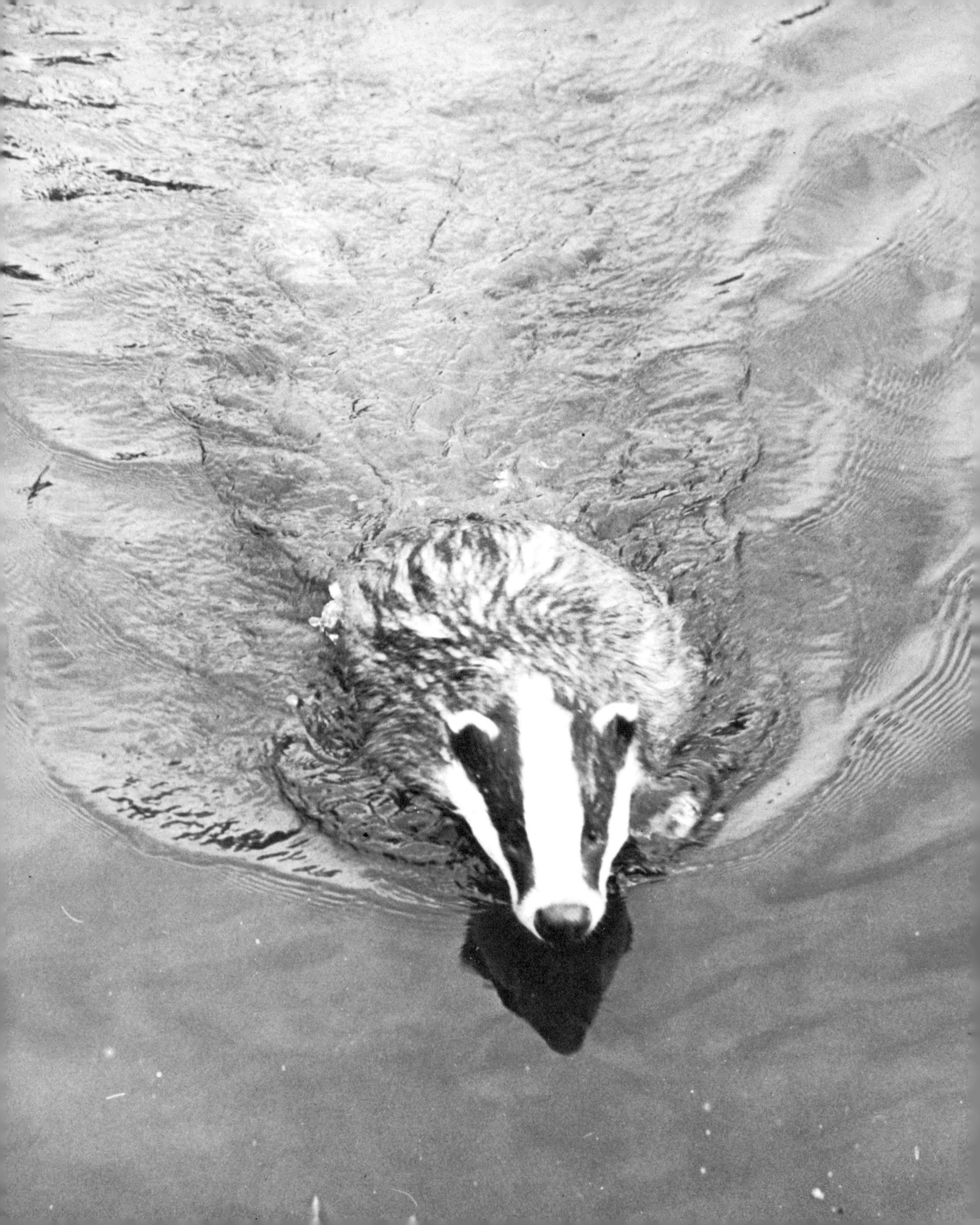

Above and left: Badgers can also swim—if they have to!

badgers chase and fight each other, and run about in a mad way. They give off scent from the gland beneath their tails. Finally they mate outside the set.

The young are born in February or March of the next year. This means that the time from mating to birth, the gestation period, is about seven months. This is a very long time indeed for an animal the size of a badger. The gestation period in the fox, for example, is only about seven weeks. In man, much bigger than the badger, it is nine months. Why then does it take so long for the badger to develop from the egg to the new-born cub?

The long gestation period is due to what is called *delayed*

A badger proceeds warily, sniffing the ground as he goes.

implantation. To see what we mean by this, we must first explain what happens during the early growth of other mammals.

Just before mating, the female's ovaries release eggs which pass into the womb, or *uterus*, in which the animal will grow before being born. The eggs wait there to be

Badgers are peaceful animals, and don't fight when they meet their badger neighbours.

fertilized by the sperm injected into the uterus by the male during mating. At the same time, the ovaries also send out hormones, or chemical messengers, into the blood. These reach the uterus and tell it to make ready to receive the fertilized egg. The sides of the uterus become spongy and its blood flow goes up. In a day or so, the fertilized egg

Once they mate, they stay together for life.

attaches itself to the wall of the uterus; straight away it gets food and oxygen from the uterus, and the little embryo starts to grow. In other words, the fertilized egg *implants* into the uterus. Later the growing embryo gets its food and oxygen through a special organ called the placenta.

But in the badger, the ovary sends out no messages to

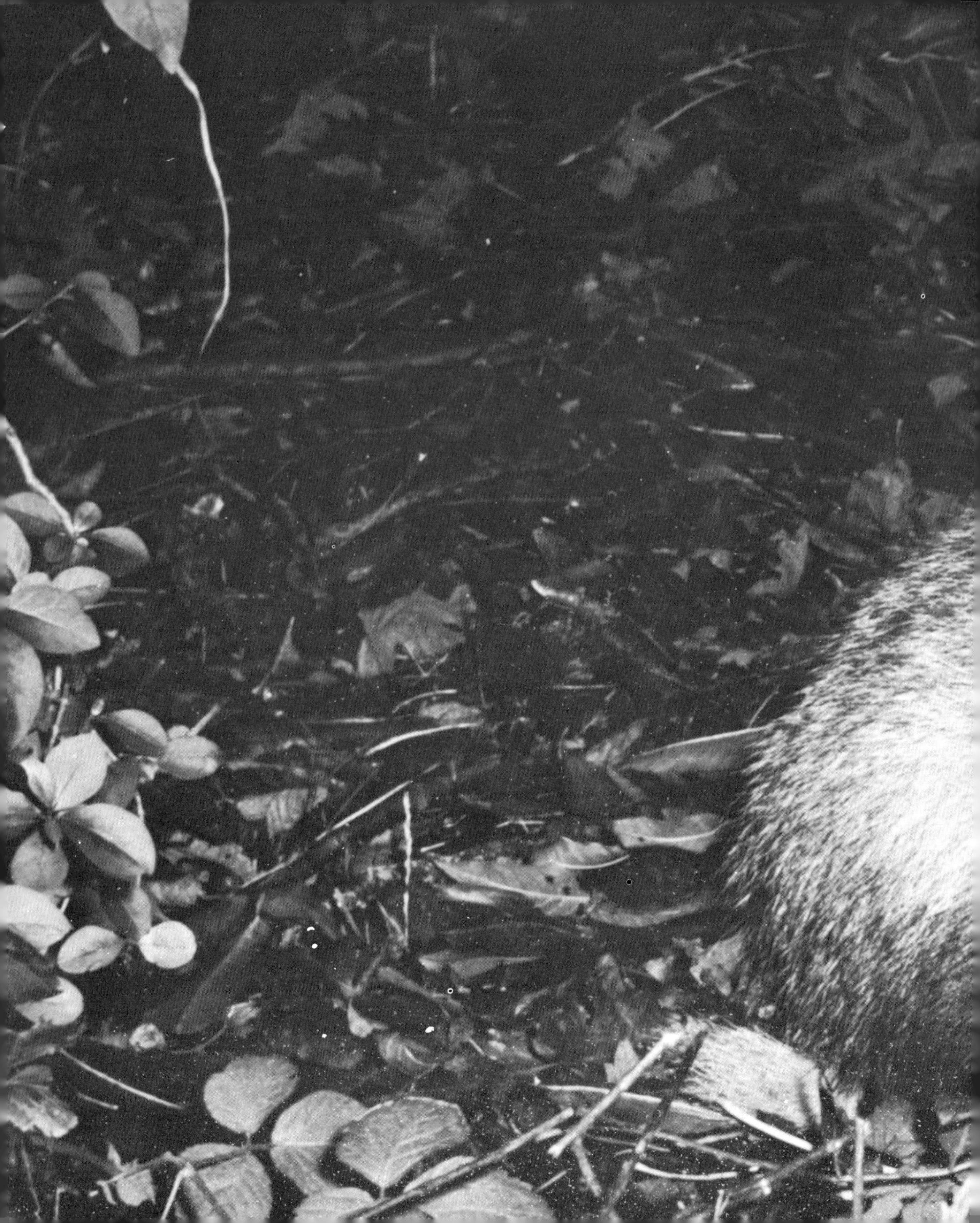

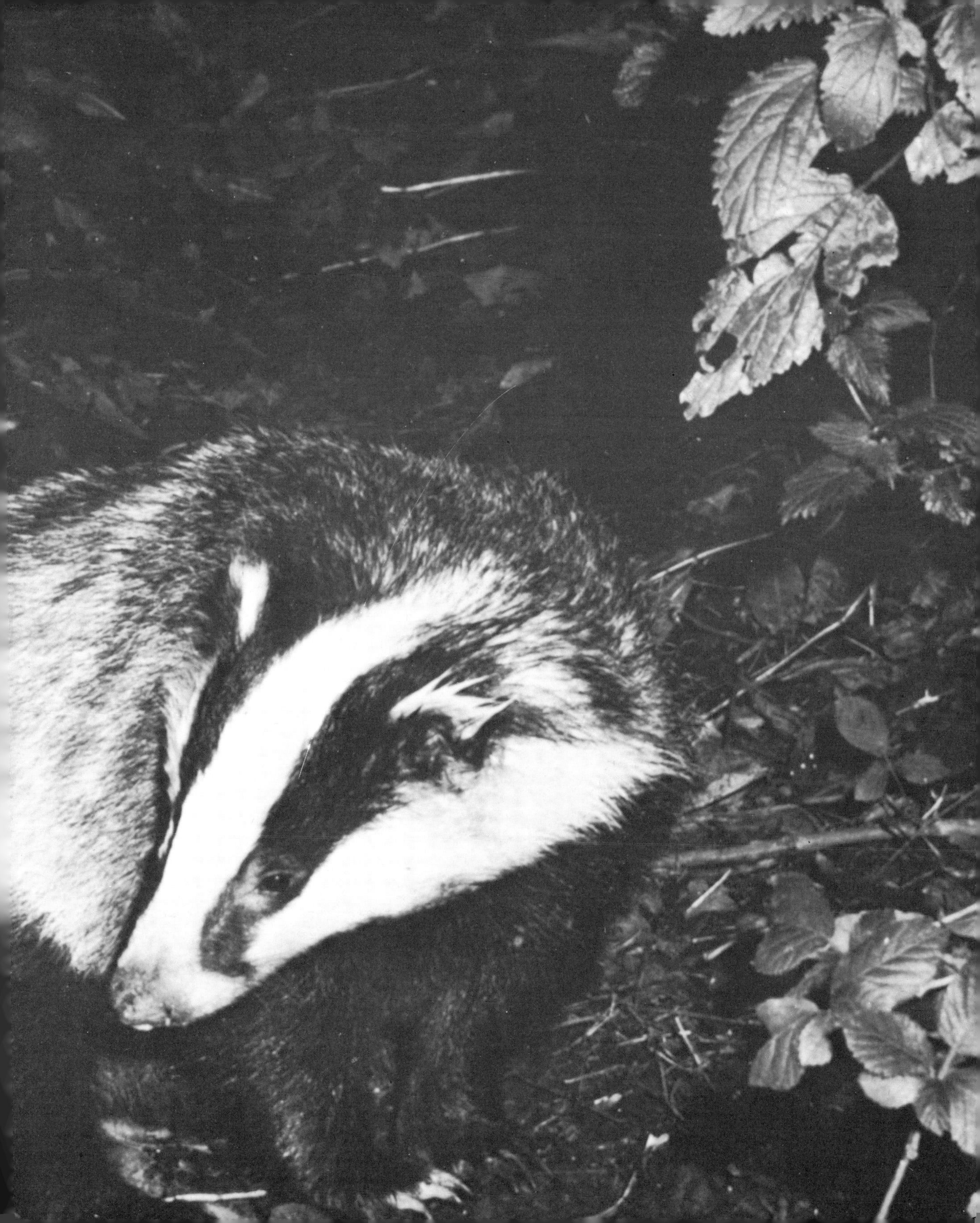

Above and right: Badgers live mostly in woodland and other areas where there are few people about; but they still move along cautiously and are always on the alert for any strange smell.

the uterus until about five months after mating. The fertilized egg, about three millimetres long, does not attach to the wall, but floats about in the uterus during this time. So implantation is delayed for about five months. Since the embryo is not attached to the uterus, it can get no food or oxygen from the mother and so it doesn't grow. It can only start growing when it is implanted. From then on it develops normally until birth about six weeks later.

Why is there delayed implantation in the badger? We have seen that the young are born in the spring. This is an ideal time for birth, since it gives the cubs a whole year

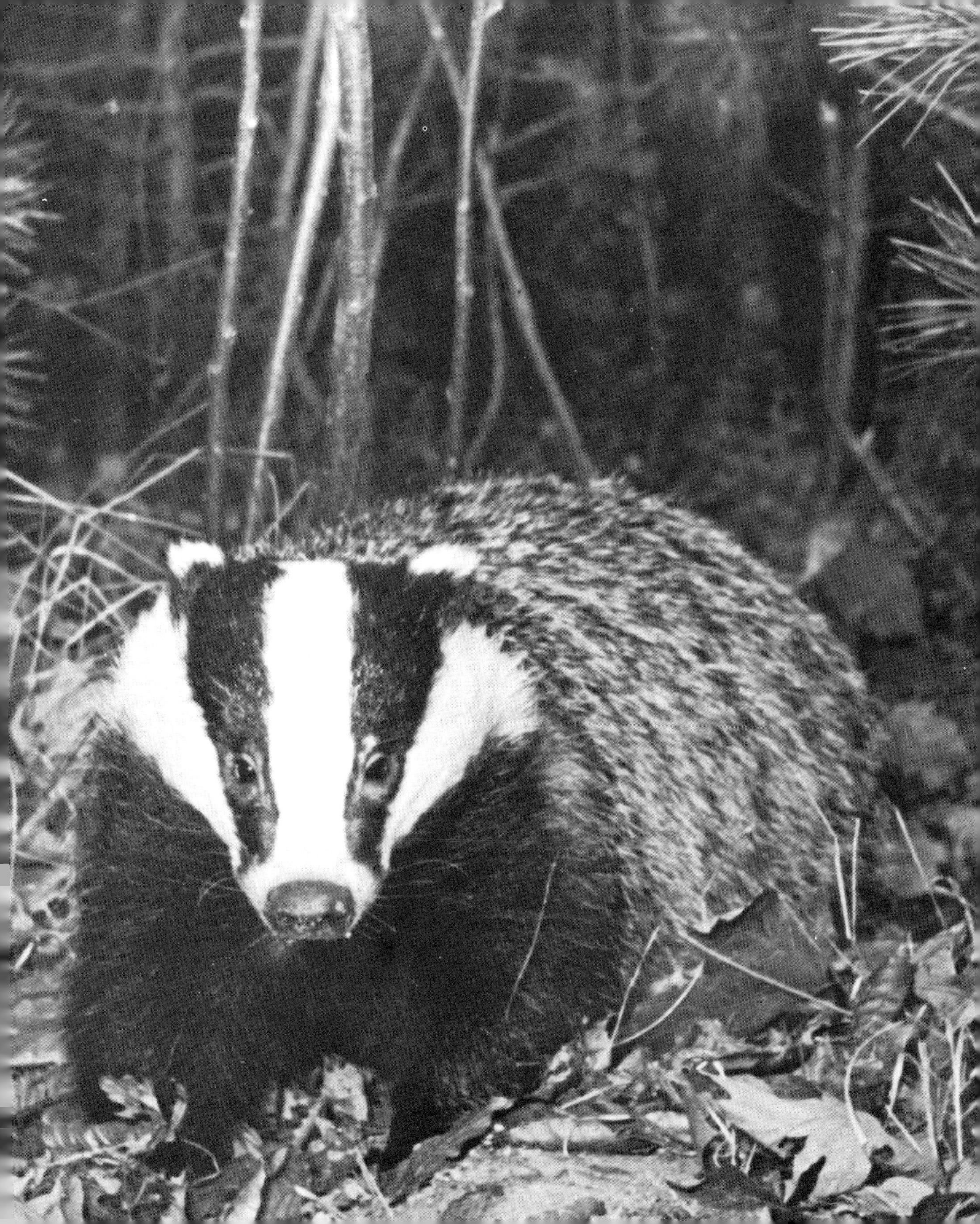

Mating

before they have to face their first winter. But we have just seen that it takes about six weeks for a badger's embryo to develop. This means that if the egg were implanted straight after mating, for birth in spring, then mating would have to be about six weeks before birth, in the middle of winter. But there is a lot of excitement during mating, and during the winter the badgers are weak and cold, and they like to stay underground for as long as possible.

So delayed implantation gets over this difficulty. The badgers can mate in the summer, when they are most active, and the growth of the embryo is held up several months, so that the cubs can be born in spring.

Among the carnivores, not only badgers delay implantation; bears, otters, and some kinds of weasels and stoats do so too.

Right: A mother with her month-old cub.

5: Family Life

In this chapter, we shall see what a typical pair of badgers do throughout the year. Both the seasonal weather and the birth of the young affect the badgers' calendar.

Family Life

Family Life

In January the badgers stay in their sets for most of the time; there is little food about and they live on their body-fat. They come out from time to time, especially on warm nights. Moonlight tends to keep them underground. When they do go out at this time of year, they seem very shy and nervous. The boar comes out first and the sow follows. The pair clear out old bedding and replace it with fresh material, for the sow will soon give birth.

Two or three cubs are born in each litter. Their bodies are about twelve centimetres long and their tails another three or four centimetres; they weigh about three ounces. Their fur is dirty white, and there are no black stripes on the head yet. These stripes are usually to be seen when the eyes open about ten days later. During this time, usually in March, the cubs' bedding is changed.

The sow stays with her cubs for long periods, suckling them, while the boar goes out a lot. The cubs' tongues are specially fitted for suckling; their edges curl up to form tubes through which the teat can be sucked. Like many other carnivores, the cubs push against their mother with their front paws to make her give milk. This is called the "milk tread."

By the end of March the cubs are ready to go outside for the first time. From then till July the cubs grow to be almost as big as their parents. This is a period of learning as well as growing. The mother leads them out of the set; she licks them and herself clean, getting rid of parasites. At first

Left: A young badger makes a strange discovery.

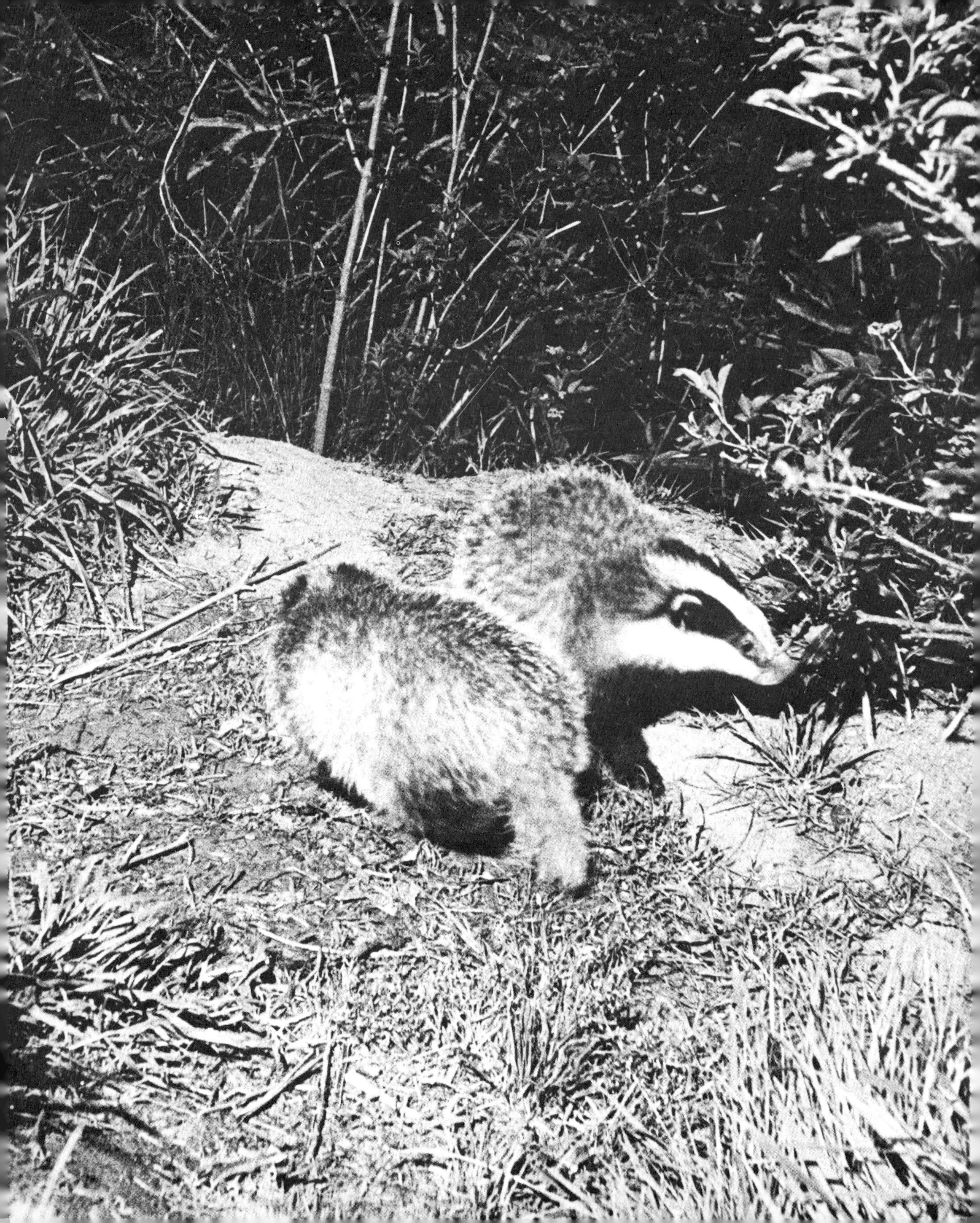

the cubs are shy and stay close to the sow.

By May the cubs play boisterously with each other and with their mother. They squeal and yelp as they fight and leap about. In between times of play the sow teaches them how to fetch bedding material, and they practice digging holes. They also learn to use the dung pits around the set. They go out feeding with their parents and learn the smells of food, and where to find it.

The mating period, as we have seen, is between July and mid-September. At this time the pair of badgers become even more excited than usual. They go off to their favourite playgrounds in their area; their romping flattens big patches of plants. Sometimes they may flatten corn in this way, but the damage they do is never very great. Sometimes they play in trees with thick, low, branches too.

After mating, the pair and their cubs may leave the set and go to another, sharing it with two or three other families. Before going they clean out the old set so that when they go back to it in the autumn it will be fresh and clean.

By October the big cubs usually leave their parents for good and set up on their own. The mated pair start to make their own set ready for the winter. They collect up bedding on dry nights until the end of November to line the chambers. The badgers do not play much by this time, but they still come out on most nights.

From November to January the weather is at its

Left: Two young badgers frolic outside the entrance to their set.

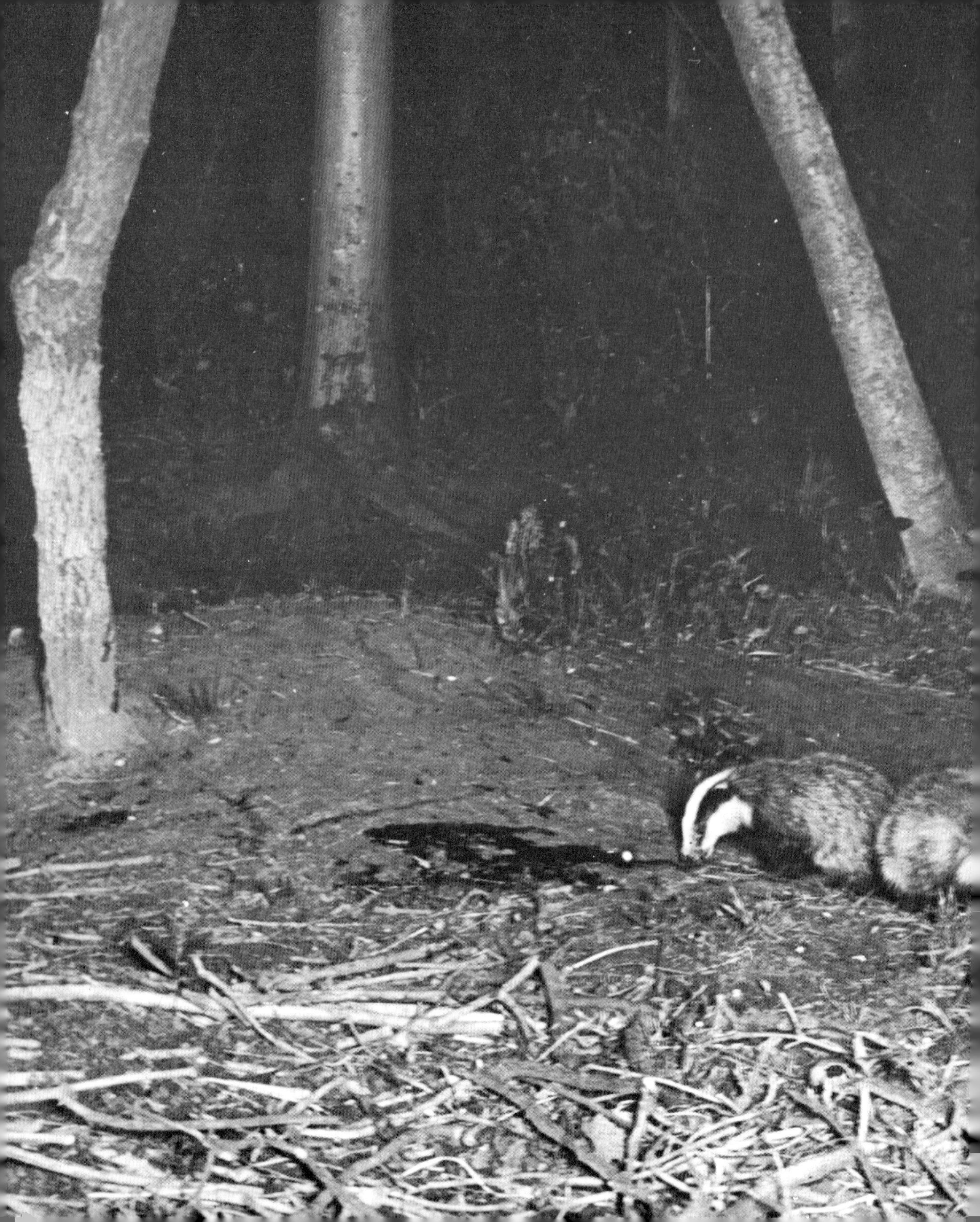

A family of badgers at night by their set in the woods.

Family Life

worst. People have often said that badgers hibernate during the winter. True hibernation is only found in a few mammals. Mammals are warm-blooded – they keep their body-temperature high and steady no matter what the outside temperature. But a hibernating mammal, when winter comes, lets its temperature drop to that of the air. It slows down the workings of its body so that its heart beat and breathing become very slow, and it goes into a deep sleep. Hedgehogs hibernate like this, but badgers don't. Although they are sluggish and stay in their sets for up to three days at a time during the winter, they are still active. You can often see fresh dung in the dung pits and tracks in the snow at this time of year.

By mid-January the pair are once again preparing the set for the new litter of cubs.

Examining an inviting hole...

... and coming out satisfied.

6: Badgers and Man

Apart from disease, Man is the European badger's only enemy. The badger has been persecuted for a long time. During the seventeenth and eighteenth centuries, parishes in the Lake District paid out sixpence or a shilling for every badger caught. One of these parishes paid for the death of seventy-three badgers in eight years.

Even today badgers are seen as a nuisance by many farmers and gamekeepers. But in fact badgers do more good by feeding on insect pests than they do harm. Many badgers are killed by shooting or baiting with poisoned food; or the sets may be filled with cyanide gas, or simply dug out and the badgers inside killed. In sandy soil the badger can dig away faster than his hunters can dig themselves. So terriers may be sent down into the set; the dog is trained to bite the badger every time it tries to dig, but leaps back away from the badgers jaws.

Why is the badger thought to be harmful? As we have seen, badgers may tread down corn when they play, or may dig small temporary sets in fields. Badgers may also attack poultry, but this is very, very rare; chicken feathers

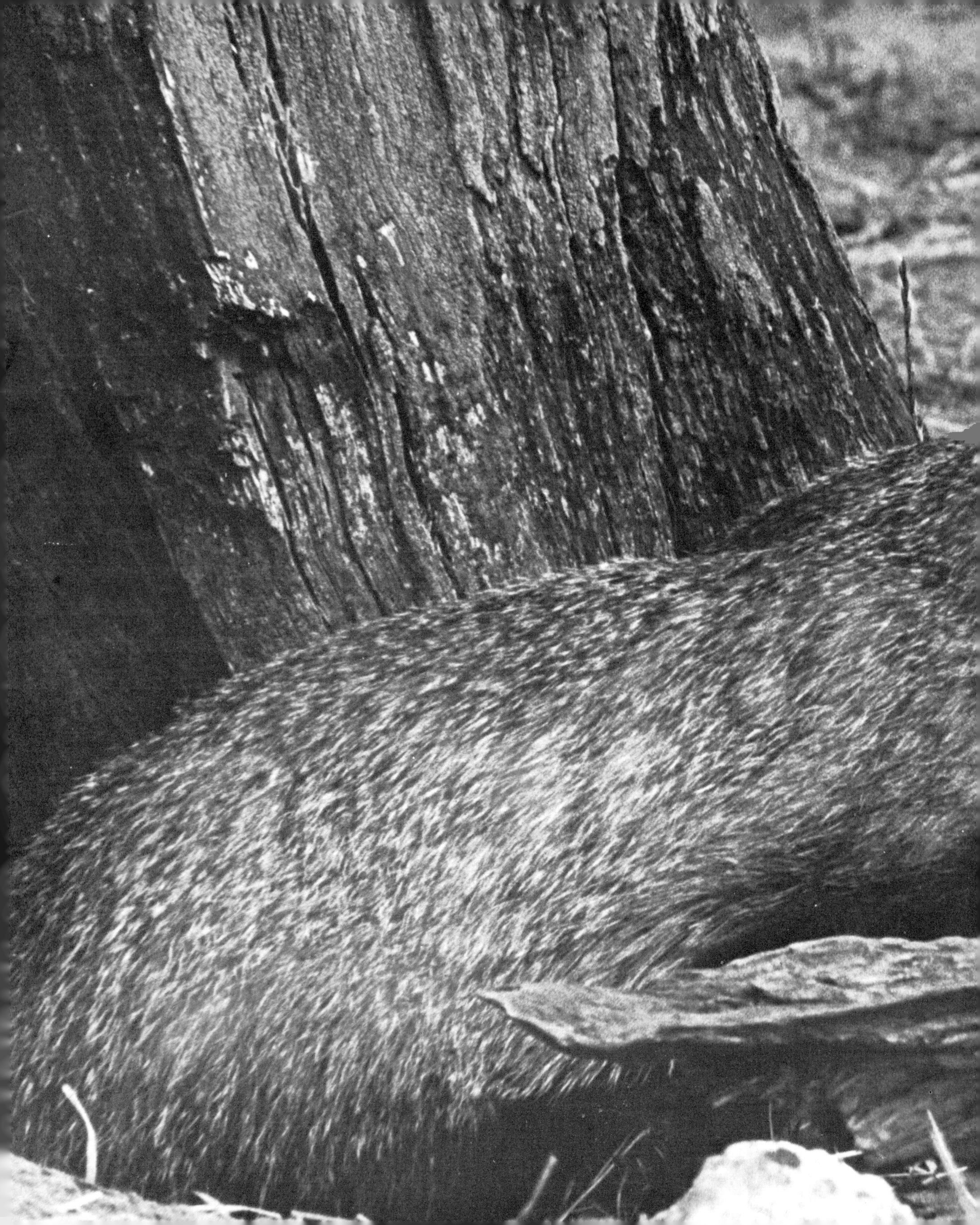

Daylight dawns, and the badger takes a last look before retiring to bed.

Above: Badgers travel well-used badger paths, some of them hundreds of years old.

near the set are usually due to foxes which may be using the set as an earth. Young pheasants too may be eaten by badgers. But the total damage that badgers do is really very small, and they do not deserve to be killed just for this.

Badgers are also killed for sport. An especially cruel sport is badger baiting, which still goes on today. A badger is dug out of its set, using a terrier as described above. It is then chained up and one or two dogs set loose on it. Both badger and dogs end up badly mauled.

Below: The boy handles his badger carefully. They don't often make good pets.

Badgers and Man

Badgers and Man

Badgers do not like dogs and will bite any that come too near. It is best to keep them apart.

Badgers and Man

Badgers have few commercial uses. Badger fat is still used for the treatment of rheumatism and other ailments in some places. The animal's fur is used for making expensive shaving brushes. Very seldom do people eat badger meat as a delicacy.

However, it seems that the badger is holding its own, at least in Great Britain. But this state of affairs can only be kept up if we remind people that badgers are harmless, interesting animals, and well worth looking after.

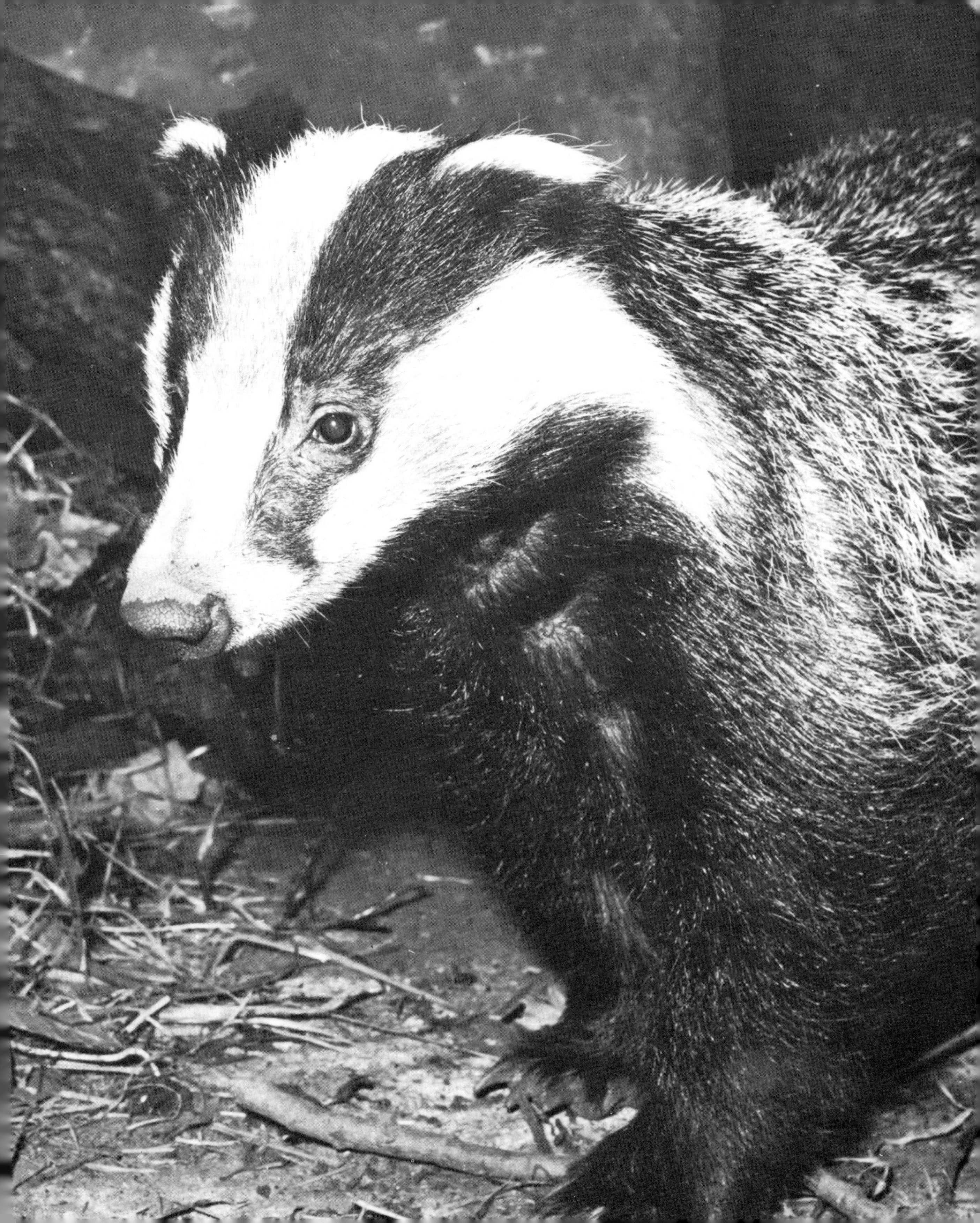

Glossary

BEDDING. Material, usually straw or grass, which badgers use to line the chambers in their sets.

BOAR. A male badger.

CARNIVORE. A large group of mammals, including badgers, bears, cats, dogs and seals, most of which feed on living animals.

CARNIVOROUS ANIMAL. One which eats only animal food.

COUNTERSHADING. The colouring worn by an animal to even out the brightness of its coat for the purposes of camouflage; the back of the animal is darker than the underside.

DEFENCE MECHANISM. The means by which an animal makes itself dangerous or unpleasant to an attacker, e.g. by sting, bad taste or powerful bite.

DELAYED IMPLANTATION. The way by which the growth of an animal is held up so that birth takes place in the spring.

GESTATION PERIOD. The time between mating and birth.

HIBERNATION. The deep winter sleep into which a few mammals go, when they let their body temperature drop.

IMPLANTATION. The attachment of the fertilized egg to the wall of the uterus.

MYXOMATOSIS. A disease deadly to rabbits.

OMNIVORE. An animal which eats both plant and animal food, e.g. badgers, pigs, men.

OVARY. The egg-producing organs of the female animal.

PLACENTA. The special organ through which the embryo gets food and oxygen from the mother's uterus.

SET. The underground home of the badger, with tunnels and chambers.

SOW. A female badger.

UTERUS. The womb; the part of the female animal in which the embryo grows.

WARNING COLORATION. The opposite of camouflage; the striking colours worn by an animal with a defence mechanism.

Finding Out More

The best reference book on the natural history of the badger is Neal's *The Badger* in Collins' "New Naturalist" series. Neal has also written a smaller book called *Badgers*. More information about the European badger can be found in *Mammals*, by Claus König. If you want to find out more about British wild life in general you can read *British Mammals*, by Harrison Matthews.

If you live in the country you may be lucky enough to have a badger set in your neighbourhood. Small sets are best, but remember that badgers are only active at dusk and at night if you want to see them. You must remain absolutely quiet and still and make sure that the wind is blowing your scent away from the set entrance. Badgers are blind to red light, and so you can use a red torch to see them. But you must not lose patience; you may have to wait many nights before you see one!

Because they live in sets, European badgers are difficult to see in captivity. But some of the larger zoos may have other kinds of badger on show. At the London Zoo you can see Ferret and Hog Badgers.

Index

American badgers, 11, 12
ankle joints, 20, 21

badger baiting, 67, 70
badger digging, 67
bedding, 24, 59, 61, 76
body fat, 59
birth, 47, 57, 59
bite, 12, 16, 41
burial, 30

claws, 20, 22
coloration, 16, 19, 20, 76, 77
communal living, 61
cubs, 54, 59, 61, 64

defence, 16, 41
delayed implantation, 48–56, 76

disease, 24
dung pits, 24, 61, 64

Ferret badgers, 10
fleas, 24
food, 30–41, 51, 54
fossil badgers, 7
foxes, 32

gestation, 47–8, 76

hairs, 14, 16
hearing, 28
hedgehogs, 33, 41, 64
hibernating, 64, 76
Hog badgers, 10
Honey badgers, 10

mating period, 43, 47, 61
moonlight, 59

parasites, 24, 59
play, 61, 67

playgrounds, 61
poultry killing, 41, 67

rabbits, 32, 36

scent, 26, 28, 47
sets, 14, 21–8, 30, 59, 61, 64, 67, 70, 77
sight, 26
skulls, 41, 42
skunks, 7, 8, 18–19, 20
smell, sense of, 28, 30
Stinking badgers, 10
suckling, 59
summer, 56, 59, 61

teeth, 31, 32, 41

warning coloration, 16, 19, 20, 77
winter, 56, 59, 61, 64
worms, 10, 33, 36

Picture Credits

The author and publishers would like to thank the following for permission to reproduce pictures on the pages indicated: Ardea Photographics, *frontispiece*, 6, 26, 37, 40, 44–5, 51; Mary Evans Picture Library, *title page*; Pictorial Press Ltd, 7, 47; Frank W. Lane, 8, 9, 11, 13, 14, 18–19, 28, 29, 38–9, 50, 62–3, 65, 66, 68–9; Paul Popper Ltd, 10, 12, 57, 72–3; Natural History Photographic Agency, 15, 17, 20, 21, 22, 23, 25, 31, 32, 33, 34–5, 48–9, 58, 60, 70–1, 75; Heather Angel, 27, 42; Bruce Coleman Ltd, 43, 46, 52–3, 54, 55.